Missing Orion

Missing Orion

Poems by
Barbara Bloom

SHANTI ARTS PUBLISHING
BRUNSWICK, MAINE

Missing Orion

Published by Shanti Arts LLC

Designed by Shanti Arts Designs

Shanti Arts LLC
193 Hillside Road,
Brunswick, Maine 04011

shantiarts.com

Cover image— arnaud-mariat / EAG366wu-b0 / unsplash.com

Printed in the United States of America

ISBN: 978-1-962082-87-7 (softcover)

Library of Congress Control Number: 2025949360

for Fred and Kathryn

Contents

V.   From the 49th Parallel ✳

Acknowledgments

Acknowledgment is made to the following publications in which these poems first appeared, sometimes in slightly different versions:

Catamaran: "April, Pinnacles Road"; "At the Barn View Community Garden"; "At Lake Louise in October"; and "Memory of Orcas"

Examined Life: A West Washington Poets Network Anthology: "Bottom of the Vineyard" and "Bright Dream"

Porter Gulch Review: "Sailing North"

Raven Chronicles: "Salvage"

Shark Reef: "The Garden on Spring Street"

The author wishes to thank the following for their encouragement, helpful criticism, and love of poetry: Joseph Stroud and members of his ongoing workshop; the Hummingbird Poets—Len Anderson, Charles Atkinson, Wilma Marcus Chandler, Simon Hunt, Rosie King, George Lober, Maggie Paul, Kim Scheiblauer, David Sullivan, Amber Sumrall, and Ken Weisner; my Santa Cruz zoom writing group—Rosie King, Wilma Marcus Chandler, and Susan Freeman; and Bellingham poet Richard Widerkehr.

Many thanks to Christine Cote of Shanti Arts for her enthusiastic support and for making this book happen. I am deeply grateful to Ellery Akers and Paula Jones for a lifetime of friendship and shared writing. For steadfast loving support, thank you to my family—my daughter, Kathryn Gailson, and grandsons, Galil and Hanokh Gailson, my sister, Elizabeth Ramstead, and my brother, Carl Bloom, and his wife, Diane Zipperman. And my husband, Fred Winterbottom, whose love has allowed me to take root and bloom.

I.

Shadow and Sun

✦ ✦ ✦ ✦ ✦

.

My Mother's Kitchen

Spaghetti sauce bubbles on the stove,
the wooden spoon dipped in
decisively by my mother
for a quick judicious taste—
then some small adjustment, more salt,
a bit more dried oregano.

Perched on the three-step ladder,
I crunch a stick of raw spaghetti,
knowing I'm just a visitor here.

She puts the big pot of water on,
adds the spaghetti,
the lid adjusted at just a slight tilt
so it won't boil over, but then my father
bursts in, wanting to know how much longer till dinner,
and the calm of the kitchen is ruffled,
like a sudden wind disturbing the surface of a lake.
"Well, why aren't you helping?"
he wants to know, glaring my way
on his way out.

The air is heavy
with the good scent of tomatoes and basil,
and I can hear the splat of boiling water
hitting the metal lid of the pot
like it always does.
All of this would seem to be saying,
Everything is fine!
Just look at this happy scene!
but I don't believe it
though I want to.

Father to Daughter

he brought us to the unfinished house
on the private estate of people
he knew slightly
my mother had made a picnic
and spread a blanket under a huge live oak
its branches offering some shade

the house was a wedding present
he told us
father to daughter
you could see it was grand
though it was just the skeleton of a house

the daughter had killed herself
the night before the wedding
and construction was halted
the very next day

why was he so drawn to this place
that was a mystery and so much
missing from the story
as it was from our own

I imagined the girl
must have loved someone else
and would rather die
than marry the man
her father had chosen

my mother passed around the sandwiches
cheese on thick French bread
a hawk circled overhead
its red tail catching the sun

look my father said
pointing upwards
there was going to be an elevator
imagine that
an elevator in your house

Swim Lessons

Stanford University, 1958

It was important to learn "Dead Man's Float"
and from there the crawl, sidestroke,
backstroke, treading water, holding your breath
underwater for a full minute.
After an hour, soggy and smelling of chlorine,
my brother and I would explore the campus,
waiting for our father to get off work
at the School of Mining.

We'd sit on perfect lawns in front of fountains
and eat our peanut butter and tomato sandwiches—
sometimes we'd venture to The Cellar
and sit in the dim light,
watching the college students
laughing at their tables, talking, drinking coffee or beer.
So this is what grown-up looks like!

A walk through the sandstone arches
would bring us to our father's lab,
where we'd descend a cement stairway
into the cool space smelling of chemicals.
He'd be there, standing over beakers,
or putting things away in tall cupboards.

Then at five o'clock
we'd climb into the old open-air Jeep
our wet suits rolled up in towels,
and cling to its sides while our father drove home,
the way he always did, accelerating wildly
on the hairpin turns up Old La Honda Road.

When we reached the gate,
one of us would jump out with the key
and swing the heavy gate open—the world
of the college kids, books tucked under their arms,
a girlfriend or a boyfriend strolling through the sun,
gone—as the gate was closed,
the padlock snapped shut.

Understanding the Land of Jerky

What you need to know is
we had our own country—
and on the rare occasions
our parents went out, leaving us alone,
we'd hold our secret council meetings.

Feet on the kitchen table,
dining on cracker and butter sandwiches,
each one made with a whole sleeve of saltines,
washed down with generous glasses of 7-Up,
we made our own laws.

My brother, being oldest, was king,
my sister and I his willing subjects.
The laws said there were no rules.
Vegetables were nonexistent,
especially canned peas,
which my sister hated,
and bedtime was past midnight.
Bouncing on beds was allowed.
In fact, it was required!

My brother drew the maps
on tracing paper, the same paper
he used for drawing the maps of Europe
before and after World War II. Only here,
he had more scope. Our country was vast,
filled with rivers and mountains,
forests, castles, glittering cities.

When we heard our parents opening the front door,
we rolled up the maps, brushed off the crumbs,
and hurried to our beds. What
we never said, even to each other,
was that one day, we were going to really escape.

Our parents would never find us.
No one would. We'd live in our own country,
ill-nourished, utterly happy.

In Walford's Garden

While the adults sat inside, talking,
we roamed the garden—
the bridges and curving paths making it enormous,
a place we could happily be lost in. Sometimes Walford—
deeply tanned from his years of sailing the South Seas—
would step outside and wave hello.

We'd never heard of Eden— the Bible
forbidden in our atheist house—
so it wasn't until much later I realized I'd been there,
in that unfallen world, not knowing a single plant by name,
but knowing in another way
that this garden held everything of happiness,
and that I would try in my own gardens, all my life,
to approach this.

Pulling out periwinkle plants,
whose tough stems cut my hands,
yanking up Bermuda grass
with its intricate nodules and intertwined roots,
and digging holes for bareroot roses
or narcissus bulbs that were dry and brown,
the soil on my hands still cold with winter,
I'd stand up to stretch—and I'd be back there,
where the Belle of Portugal roses
hung from arbors flush with scent,
where my legs would brush
the geraniums, lavender, and zinnias
as I walked along those paths
he'd carved out in his small plot of land:
everything saying *there is more,*
there is always more, believe in this.

With Winter Coming On

Skyline, California, 1958

That fall we dug a bomb shelter—
hard going in the dry soil of California—
my brother had the plans
from his *Popular Mechanics* magazine,
the finished shelter on the cover:
happy family seated at a table,
safely below ground,
enjoying a snack, a board game,
canned goods stored neatly on a shelf,
while outside, bombs fell,
the world was ending.

Called in to dinner,
we'd return tired,
our hands hastily washed,
to sit stiffly at the table
where talking was not allowed,
and shoot glances at each other
over our Melmac plates,
knowing we were building something
outside, getting ready for winter,
preparing for the worst.

At the Sills' Ranch

Skyline Boulevard, 1959

in the morning we drank goats' milk
laced with coffee
out of thick pottery mugs
made by your parents
and your mother spoke to us
as if we weren't children
but her equals

after breakfast
we scattered the belled goats with a wave of our hands
racing to the pasture where the horses waited
and climbing onto their bare backs
we urged them into a canter
warm air rushing against our faces

in that moment everything
our lives would hold
stretched before us as easily
as the rutted one-lane road we took
winding through coyote brush and live oaks
down to the main highway
where I'd turn my horse for home
and you'd head back the way we came
with just a quick wave goodbye

My Mother's Backpacking Journal, 1960

Remember what it was to be me: that is always the point.
—Joan Didion, "On Keeping a Notebook"

As in her life, it's what's left out,
what's not said, that I long for—
not the careful notation of each day's miles,
how much our packs weighed,
or what she cooked,
yes, the good wife, the dutiful mother
is here, but where is *she*,
separate from this,
say standing on a mountain pass,
looking down to a green valley,
or wet through, after a surprise afternoon thundershower,
her shirt sticking to her back,
with miles to go before the next camp
and a hot meal,
which she will have to prepare,
bending over the campfire—
but here, the perfect handwriting
never wavers, the bare descriptions
"beautiful hike, delectable eastern brook trout,"
a code I can't break, and the person
I always wanted to know
not revealed, hidden as a deer
in mottled light.

Posing with Grandfather

My brother and I are standing on our toes
as we lean for balance against the VW bug,
competing to be tallest. My sister
stands squarely on her feet,
Grandfather's arm draped around her.

We are dressed up, my sister and I
in matching outfits, my brother in a sports coat,
so perhaps the picture was taken when Grandfather
was leaving. I remember little of his visit
except that we would sometimes
work for him, making his bed, washing his dishes,
and be paid in shiny quarters. I was sure
he must be full of stories,
and I begged him to tell me about "the olden days,"
but he scarcely talked to us.
I don't remember him ever smiling.

And looking at the photo now, I can see
he's already back on his farm in Indiana,
where things make better sense.
For here, his grandchildren call their parents
by their first names,
and run around naked and unshod
under the too-blue skies of California.
And they won't even pose properly
in this picture he will likely carry home.

Breaking Open a Bale of Alfalfa

The nylon strings severed,
the bale pops open,
densely packed green
a few purple flowers—
the smell of summer,
the smell of before-we-left.

The green stable,
a little ramshackle,
poison oak encroaching,
its viney tendrils
breaking through the siding,
and just outside, the stalks of cow parsnip
towering over me.
Two stalls.
My horse Blitzen in one,
munching his dinner,
I in the other,
sitting on an unopened hay bale,
listening to his matter-of-fact horse sounds,
sighs, tail swishings, stomping of hooves,
not wanting to leave, ever,
and walk up to the house—

though I didn't know then,
this would soon become
a place I would visit
only in memory—
the prickle of the hay
as I pulled a flake free.

I can still feel it
on my hands.

Childhood Allowance

You didn't allow us "Father" or "Dad,"
only your first name, Gil.
"Gil, like a fish," you'd say,
chuckling at your own joke.
It was to bridge the age gap,
you explained, since you were old
for a father, and to keep yourself
from abusing your power.

You must have known
that was a danger. Only what's clear now
is that you were the child,
and to us, your children,
fell the task of keeping you happy,
putting aside our own wishes for yours,
sometimes handing back our shiny silver dollars
if you saw something you wanted
and had run short of cash—
a book or maybe a bunch of bananas.

If I could, I'd reach back
to the frightened children we were,
trying so hard to be good—
and I'd hand out silver dollars,
lots of them,
and say, "Spend these
however you like!
You've earned them!
They're yours!"

Shadow and Sun

"He's blocking your sun," the astrologer says,
  pointing at the chart he's drawn,
  when I tell him my father and I aren't close.
"No," he says, "it's not that you're not close,
  but that you're too close. His Saturn's
  overshadowing your Leo sun."

Now, years after my father's death,
  I remember the feeling of suffocation:
  I'm twelve, lying in bed, struggling to breathe,
  the asthma squeezing my chest,
  and my father looking down at me, says,
"Sunshine! Sunshine, that's the cure!"
  as he takes away the pills from the doctor,
  ordering me to go outside
  and take off my clothes. "Let
  the sun do its work!" He will
  boast of this later to his friends.

From this distance in time, it's impossible
  not to see the shadow he cast over me for so long,
  like an eclipse, inescapable
  as it eats away the brightness,
  slowly, bit by bit—
  but unable, in the end, to hold back
  the gradual, sure return of the light.

My Mother at the Potter's Wheel

she slapped down the wet clay
and cupped it in her hands
as the wheel whirred and turned
and the lump of clay
began to take shape

I'd just stopped by
on my way to see my horse
a carrot in my pocket for him
but I couldn't seem to leave
this sight of my mother
her hair falling across her face
as she bent down
deeply concentrating

nothing to do with us
her children or our father
under whose shadow
she usually disappeared
but not here
in an old shirt messy with clay

sun outside on the live oaks
and my ten-year-old-self leaning against the wall
invisible to her
the clay under her hands
growing into a bowl
as if nothing else mattered
only this

Not Drawing

Because the horses I drew in my notebooks were lumpy,
not the creatures I saw in my mind—
manes and tails flowing as they galloped by,
dark eyes like pools you could slip into for hours,
sweet curve of the shoulder, of the rump—
at eleven, I quit drawing.

For, looking out the car window
as we passed by horses in the fields,
I felt their graceful forms in my own body
when they stepped from sunlight into shade
or bent their necks down, swanlike,
to graze on the grass
that, by loving them so completely,
I could also taste: green, cold.

But I couldn't draw this perfection.

That was before I began writing,
before I learned to be glad of even a glimpse
of the form in mind, be it horse, tree, or human,
to be grateful for even the clumsy, lopsided efforts
my words, like the stubby elementary school pencils,
were trying to draw.

The Garden at Skyline

I thought I was taming the garter snakes
when I'd scoop them up,
stroke them, and talk to them
in the neglected rose garden.
They'd dart their tongues out at me—
I took this for a form of language,
and when they squirmed in my hands,
I let them go.

Sometimes I'd climb into the ornamental cherry tree
and sit in a fork in the branches,
picking the double pink blossoms,
tucking them behind my ears.
They were like the tissue paper flowers
we'd make in school—that crinkled, that delicate.

I can't really enter that time
as I'd like to, go back and be that skinny girl
with the long braids flopping down her back.
I don't know anymore
what it felt like being eight or ten,
but I wonder if even then,
even from outside the house, I could feel
the presence of my father,
upstairs in his room,
propped on his sitting-up-in-bed pillow,
reading, the fluorescent lamp buzzing over his head,
waiting for his dinner, and my mother,
busy in the kitchen, putting the last touches
on a meal we would eat in silence.

What I know is that I didn't want
to leave the garden,
where the snakes with their elegant orange stripes
were always to be found,
and as the light dimmed, the deer would wander through
to nibble the rose petals,
coming so near I might have touched them.

Locked Gate

I don't have a key
though everything here is familiar.
I remember opening the gate so many times
as a child, the stiffness of the padlock,
the word "Master" stamped across it,
metallic smell of the chain, the sharp click
as it sprang open, then dragging the heavy gate
and leading my horse through
before closing it behind me.

The trees knew me then,
and the wide turns on the way to the house
littered with the musky tassels of tanbark oaks,
the impossibly small cones of the redwoods.
I remember the sticky monkey flowers
that grew along the road, gold as my favorite crayon.
Once I picked a bouquet for my mother,
and my fingers stuck together
as I held it out to her.

My mother, dead now for so many years,
the property sold long ago, divided up,
the old metal gate gone—but still
I stand there, in the dream,
waiting to be let inside.

Dear Life

for my brother and sister

We'd play *run run run till you can't touch the ground*
till it grew so dark out we'd stub our bare toes
on the tree roots sticking up
as we made our bold dashes, clutching
the rope swing, and hanging on
for dear life, as we liked to say,
gripping the knots in the rope with our cold hands,
and then, suddenly, we'd be off the ground—
whoosh!—in the air,
not even caring that in seconds
we'd be bumping back across the hard ground,
trying to stop ourselves with our feet—
no, the moment in the air
made it worth everything!

Then in the distance, our mother's voice
calling us in, and how dark it was
walking back towards the lighted windows
for dinner, where we'd sit
stiff in our places, no talking allowed,
our faces still flushed from flying.

Bright Dream

for Rosie

Having printed out my poem
of running from my father,
I see on the back of the page
one of your poems: there are your parents,
in a dream, bending over you
tenderly. You will be safe and loved.
Your mother's diamond ring
flashes above you.

I long to turn the page,
trade my story
for yours. To shake out
this darkness,
as easily as one shakes
crumbs from a blanket
after a picnic,
fold the blanket,
smell the sunshine in my arms.

II.

The Wilds of Canada

✦ ✦ ★ ✦ ✷

Sailing North

San Francisco, California, to Galley Bay, British Columbia

The masts waved between the stars
as if trying to connect them,
like the dot-to-dot pictures
I'd loved as a child—
where a scattering of numbers
suddenly emerged as a lion,
an ice cream cone, or a house—
only that childhood on land
seemed a million miles away now,
as I gripped the tiller, trying
to hold the boat steady on course.

My brother beside me in the cockpit,
looking serious, younger than his sixteen years,
his face barely showing
through the hood of his yellow foul weather gear:
it was our watch,
four hours, 2 a.m. to 6 a.m.
Spray blew back at us,
and he poured out
some coffee from the Stanley thermos
and passed it over to me,
the hot metal cup burning
first my hands, then my tongue.
I stared at the swinging compass
heading us north,
away from everything known,
familiar, loved.

The boat bucked its way forward,
and we sat there,
talking to stay awake.

Blackberry Time

We wouldn't have known it then,
but when we plucked the berries
from the thorny vines
and popped them in our mouths,
amazed they could be so sweet, so warm,
we might as well have been
signing a pact, just as our parents,
back in the house, were signing their names
to paper, to buy the place.

On that first walk
through the apple orchard,
heading towards the steep trail
for a view of the whole property,
our hands stained with dark juice
mixed with blood from the thorns,
we'd as good as pledged:
We will always take care of you.
We will always love you.

For though we'd battle the vines—
in the flower beds, vegetable garden, the orchard,
overtaking everything—
they bound our lives in toil,
in sweetness, to the place,
the very earth itself—as they do still.
So that any blackberry,
whether on the old homestead, or anywhere else,
calls back that first taste
all those years ago
under a blue summer sky, a generous sun,
by which all else must be measured.

Ghost

first year at Galley Bay

I never told anyone
how night after night
I'd leave my cramped room
in the house we'd just moved into
with its worn wallpaper
showing fishermen in slickers
holding up lanterns
my own flickering kerosene lamp
making the room even darker
full of shadows
wind outside pushing up waves
I couldn't see but could hear
hitting the rocks below

it would happen without
my meaning it to
I'd be in my bed at Galley Bay
waiting for sleep
then without warning
I'd be there at the front door
of our old house on Skyline
push it open and walk in

it seemed no one had moved in
after we'd left
everything
just as it had been

so room by room
I'd walk through
heavy chairs and pale Persian rug
in the front hall
then my brother's room
big wooden radio by the bed

and down the long hallway to the room
I'd shared with my sister
and finally my parents' room at the end
with its small stucco fireplace
and the rocking chair
where my mother
would sit after dinner
reading to us from *Heidi*
or *Black Beauty*
and once past the kitchen
down the stairs
to the basement
its cold string of rooms
the servants' quarters
cement floors
cheerless bathroom
tub in one narrow room
toilet in another

I'd trail my hands
along the walls
touching the chairs
empty now
the bedcovers
rumpled as if
someone had just gotten up
and stepped out
for a moment

my eyes lingering
over everything
to remind myself
it was still there
even if I was gone
and far away

and leaving an imprint
or trying to
as ghostlike I passed through
each night

Joyce Parker

When I met you,
I was glad I was wearing my new pajamas
and just sitting at the breakfast table,
not expecting anything to happen.

Then you burst in the kitchen door,
saying you'd heard there were new people here,
and you had come to meet us.
You lived across the inlet, you said,
at Parker Harbour.

I knew right away
you would be my friend in this place,
and show me
how a girl could live
with deep water all around,
and islands covered in dark trees,
while in their secret places,
the bear slept through the dark winters.

I ran upstairs to pull on my jeans
and walk back with you
to where you'd left your rowboat.
When I came back downstairs,
you were having a cup of coffee
with evaporated milk in it,
and you and my mother were talking
like two people equal in knowledge
and in wisdom.

Remembering Winter

December 1961

It was our first real taste of winter—
the darkness and chill in the old house,
our breath white against the early morning air
as we made our way to the woodshed,
loading up each other's outstretched arms
so high we could barely see to walk,
then we'd drop them *thunk! thunk!*
into the battered woodbox in the kitchen,
where our mother would be bent over the McClary stove,
trying to coax the fire to life,
the coffee pot already set out on the burner
though it would take its time to brew.

We held our hands out to that meager warmth—
and what I see now is how young we were,
even our mother,
how far from the ease of our old lives.

We knew so little of anything—
what we'd lost, what we'd gain,
and this place we'd come to
where what mattered was the next load of wood,
or loaves rising in the warming oven,
waiting to be baked.

Our mother, different in jeans and sweaters,
not rushing off to work, but home with us,
taking quiet inventory of the pantry shelves
when she thought we weren't looking,
measuring against the days ahead.

The Other Side of the Bay

My brother, machete in hand,
slashed at the salal and sword ferns
on the narrow deer-made trail, while I followed,
trying to avoid the duff under the ancient Douglas firs—
because you could sink in up to your knees
if you weren't careful, without warning.

Once out of sight of the water,
it was easy to get turned around,
only trees, no landmarks to guide us—
and rough going through the alder patch,
where the pliant saplings slapped our faces
as we walked—*thwack! thwack!*

Finally we could see the water again,
and our house, all the way across the bay,
looking so far away.

We stepped inside the hermit's shack
as if we had a right to it—
a letter or two in faded envelopes
on the unswept floor,
a few canning jars, the rusted-out stove.
Talk was he'd lost his mind—bushed!—
and had to leave. It was easy to see why,
in that dark house, the woods at his back—
how could anyone remember
there was a world beyond this?

The damp and the ghosts drove us out,
and we decided to scramble around the rocky shore,
avoiding the woods,
for the light was fading, though it was still afternoon.

We could see smoke rising
from the chimney of our house—
I pictured the warm kitchen,
and our mother, stoking up the fire,
sitting down to roll her Bugle Boy
into a lumpy cigarette, lighting it up,
looking out the wavy glass of the front room window—
our direction—and we headed for that
like a beacon.

The Stars Will Lead You Home

of course I wanted to believe
I'd never be lost
if I followed the simple formula
my father outlined

trace a line from the cup of the Big Dipper
straight to the North Star
then knowing North
use it as a compass
for the four directions

so I leaned out over the rickety banister
of the Galley Bay house
for a better look
the chill night air biting through my thin jacket
that had been enough for California

my father standing beside me
his arm outstretched
pointing up

even then at fourteen
I was full of doubt
that it could be so easy

and longed only to slip back inside
where the rest of the family
crowded around the fireplace
reading talking
keeping warm

and having been lost
so many times since
not just in the woods
but on city streets
and in my life too

I see that this advice
like his admonition
to always follow the Scientific Principle
only believing what could be proven
which left out God
and the Easter Bunny
and lots in between

has not served me well

though the moment of my father
offering me this

what he had to offer

has remained

August, Years Later

No sign of the crocuses I planted that first winter
fifty years ago, when I thought the rain,
the dark, the long nights would never be over—
but the bulbs poked through the frost-cold earth,
and I stood there, by the creek,
my breath marking the air, amazed
at the purple and yellow buds
that were ready to unfurl, bearing their message:
no winter is without end.

No sign, either
of the nasturtiums my mother planted
in the rotten core of a fallen Douglas fir,
though the log is still here, looking almost the same,
and if I squint a little, I can see
the orange flowers spilling over the sides,
and my mother, gathering them
to garnish her salads with something pretty,
something that wasn't necessary
in a life where everything had to be of use,
had to count for something.

I keep meeting my younger self here.

The orchard is marking time more slowly,
apples ripening on trees that are over a hundred years old,
their trunks riddled with woodpecker holes,
some limbs damaged by the bears
in their yearly foray for the fruit,
but there they are—as I am—
holding out for another season.

Waking at Galley Bay

I keep looking for what has always been mine.
    —W. S. Merwin, "Variations to the Accompaniment of a Cloud"

Morning sun on the bay, horizontal lines
across the almost-still surface of the water
like a pen and ink sketch,
and then the island we never gave a name to
with its dark mantle of evergreens:
I want to imprint this
as deeply as hatchlings are said to imprint their mother,
as irreversibly. I don't know
how to tell you about loving a place
like this, never quite holding it.

The dock's ramp slopes steeply down
at low tide, creaking with the motion
of the water, and then the cry of seabirds
flying over the bay, chortle of the ravens
somewhere up in the tall firs. Each sound
separate, falling into the stillness.

I am memorizing it,
as if it were going away, or I was.
Voices drifting over the water,
the words not distinct.
Low gurgle of a bilge pump.
The sound of an anchor chain
being pulled up.

Reading Emily Carr's Journals

She seems to be writing to me
or about me, when she complains in her journal
of her "strange, set-apart life"
and how she struggles, not knowing
if she should push on or step back from her work.

Rain pounds the metal roof of my cabin,
and the boats at the dock bounce as the swells tug at them,
gray sky pressing on the slate-green bay.

Propped on the bed with pillows, my book fallen away,
I think how time slides here—
for this is the bay of my childhood,
the same sky, the one gull crying as it flies over:
no different.

The solitude I so desired presses in on me today,
hard as the sky pushing down on the water,
obscuring the edges, hiding the islands,
and the ship-destroying rocks.

I long for any sort of distraction.

Shaking the Apple Trees

Now lies the Earth all Danaë to the stars,
And all thy heart lies open unto me.
　　　—Alfred Tennyson, "Now Sleeps the Crimson Petal"

We took our places
under the heavily-burdened trees
and shook down the Early Transparent,
the Gravenstein, the King,
dodging the falling fruit,
sorry to bring down such a harvest
not for use but to rot on the ground—
but the bears had already damaged the far trees,
climbing out on the branches, breaking them,
and we were heading home that afternoon
and couldn't bring the fruit across the border,
so we stood in a rain of apples,
nothing mythical or romantic about it,
thinking only *Destroy the crop to save the trees.*
This is what it's come to.

The lines of the old poem rattling in my mind,
beautiful as they are, of no use here.

Before Tearing Down the Shed

Instead of an antique vase hidden in a corner
or a leather-bound book with a flowery inscription,
we find old bolts, mouse-chewed newspapers from 1982,
a few moldy records, scraps of wire,
and a trunk full of rusted electronic gear we can't identify
that once belonged to our father.

There's nothing worth saving here.
We toss everything on either the dump pile
or the burn pile. My brother and I don't say it,
but we both know
our father loved his stuff more than he loved us—
a hard fact callused over like the blisters
we got on our hands from sawing firewood
with the two-man Swede saw—
and it's so strange to find these ruined bits
of his life in this shed we're clearing out
so it can be demolished.

Brave Sister

As children, I was the brave sister—
oldest girl in a family where tears were mocked
and it wasn't okay to be afraid—
and you were the one
who was scared of our horse
after he bucked you off,
who hid when the thunder rumbled.
You in the house with your dolls,
me outside with our brother—
we were like two adjoining countries
with heavily guarded borders.

So now, so many years later,
sitting in the stern of your small boat
as you steer us home,
expertly maneuvering through the wakes
left by the big tourist boats,
I'm amazed at how you think nothing at all
of taking this lightweight aluminum boat
across Desolation Sound to Refuge Cove
to run a few errands.

I would be afraid without you.

You be the brave sister now,
I think, as we approach the dock at Galley Bay.
I scramble up to secure the lines—
Here, take that childhood's badge.
You pass me the bags of groceries,
and we trudge up the steep ramp to shore.

Dauntless

This is the word that comes to mind
when I think about my mother at Galley Bay
that first winter without our father, three kids, no phone,
no way to get anywhere except by boat,
which she feared.

She quietly went about making the morning fire,
baking bread, finding new ways to cook the rock cod
or red snapper we'd catch.
If she ever regretted following my father
up here, to the "Wilds of Canada,"
as he called it, or lost sleep
over what might become of us
now that he'd returned to California to work,
she never said.

When fishermen would pull into the bay
and come up to the house for a visit,
she'd offer them coffee and pie,
refill their cups, and make conversation.
The men were too polite to ask
where her husband was, or if she could manage
on her own, though the question hung in the air.

Years later, when she was old and far from this place,
my mother loved watching *Murder She Wrote*,
with its fearless heroine, a woman past middle age,
always so well-dressed, wielding a flashlight
as she entered some abandoned building,
or, with no back-up and no weapon of any kind,
scolded a killer for his foolishness.

She would have laughed at any comparison
to the bold Jessica Fletcher, but I wonder
what her thoughts might have been about her own choices,
and yes, her courage. As she tended
her pots of pansies and geraniums
on the patio of her small senior apartment—
the cord to the oxygen tank restricting her movements—
did she ever think back
to those warm loaves of bread, pulled
from the cranky woodstove oven?
Or remember the fierce winds
that battered the walls of the old house?
Did she realize—as we, her children, do—
that she was the one
who'd sustained us there in that life
from one day to the next?

Emily Dickinson by Kerosene Lamp

I see now
it was poetry
that brought me through
those first days and months in the North
when suddenly I'd lost everything
home   friends   my whole life
and the good presence
of my horse
who promised his steadiness
and I promised to always
take care of him
forever
but all that gone
and at fourteen
helpless to stop it

I sat at the desk in my room
reading
the flame flickering
as drafts blew through the window
the glass chimney black with smoke
smell of kerosene in the air
sound of our boat banging the dock
rain lashing the side of the house

but there with those poems
of garden   love   heartbreak
even death
I felt braver
as if wherever I was going
the way had already been marked

and this has been so
all these years since
my hand taken by
the hand of another
who'd gone there before
and could report back
and could sing
of it

Memory of Orcas

There they were, suddenly, just offshore,
five or six of them, leaping, arcing, splashing back down,
sleek and perfect in their black and white bodies,
but it was their *breathing* —
the huge breaths they exhaled
when they broke through the surface,
water to air, one world to another—
that we'd never forget.

Gathered on the rocky point,
we watched them, so near
we could almost touch them,
and at each breath of theirs, we'd shout out,
not even knowing we had,
as if something from deep below—
perhaps the very center of the earth—
was being brought up and revealed to us
huge and important, then gone
before we could understand
what it was.

And when finally they swam together
out into Desolation Sound
and out of our sight,
we felt the emptiness
where they had been
as we turned back to our smaller, human lives,
trying to recall
what tasks had so absorbed us
before.

III.

The Code

In Yosemite Valley, with Rilke

"Every angel is terrible," he quoted,
  as we sat on the granite boulders
  beside the Merced River swollen with snowmelt,
  shivering with the cold and something else—
  terror maybe—at the swift pull
  of desire, the inevitability of what was coming,
  his brown eyes holding mine,
  and the stars in the darkness of the mountain sky
  giant and glimmering.
                          "And are you
  terrible?" he wanted to know,
  as he pulled me to my feet,
  human, not angel at all, lost
  to the poetry, his touch,
  the river, white and noisy, over the rocks.

Special Assignment to the *Covington Virginian*

Reaching down the narrow glass necks
with long tweezers,
this man—my first interview,
though he didn't know that—assembled the hulls,
attached rigging and sails,
the running lights, one red,
one green, till the ships took form,
perfect and contained.

I wrote my notes and tried to ask
the right questions, how did he get started,
how long did each one take,
things like that. I tried not to show
how scared I felt, how young.
He was such a kind man,
I almost felt I could tell him,
not just about working for the paper,
but other things, too.

I'd always lived near the ocean,
but now in this landlocked town
enclosed by green hills,
and in a marriage,
that, new as it was,
already felt dry and wrong.
I was veering off course.

I studied the miniature ships
constructed with such care.
Waves would not
pummel them, rocks not
smash them. No seabirds
would fly past, calling out
in their harsh, commanding voices.

They would never touch water
or know wind. They would never
bring the sailor safely home.

Sheet Music

Our daughter wasn't even a year old when Frank left.
I saw him last when he came over, much later,
to collect a trunk of sheet music
left behind after his hasty exit. There was a soccer game
on the playing field as I walked him
out to his car, and kids in bright shorts
were running and shouting.

The perfect blue of Monterey Bay stretched out
below the town, and an offshore breeze
tugged at my skirt.

I held my daughter's hand
as he pried open the rusted lid of the trunk,
more interested in its contents
than in us. *How could you*
have left us? I wanted to say.
How could you do that?

Suddenly, hundreds of carpenter ants
rushed from the crumbling, ruined pages of his music,
carrying their eggs in their mouths.

A Phone Booth in Covington, Virginia, 1986

There's no magic in it, no, just myself,
feeding in some coins
to call with an ordinary message
to my once-mother-in-law:
"don't worry, we'll be a little late"—
but as I stand there in the gathering dusk,
there's his grandparents' big green house right across the street
looking as it did when I first saw it—
though they've both been dead for years,
and it's long sold—
but for a moment it's 1968, I'm twenty,
and Frank and I are walking down the street
hand in hand, legs a bit rubbery after the three-day bus ride,
and he's saying, "Just tell them you're from Canada,"
when I ask, "Do you think they'll like me?"

For, in that moment in the phone booth,
time simply dissolved,
and it was as if nothing
had happened, not our child,
not Frank's leaving, and all the years between—
and now, in the rented car,
my daughter looks my way
as I wait for his mother to come on the line,
and then her slow warm voice saying,
"You be careful driving.
  It'll be dark over the mountains."

Losing Roger to the Angels

That night we could hear the waves
even from inside the house,
where he was sitting at the piano, playing Rachmaninoff,
dark hair falling across his eyes.
On the bench beside him,
I longed to reach over and push his hair back
or take his hand, but turning to me,
out of nowhere, he said,
"Leave your daughter here
and take me to Fort Ord.
I mean to sign up for the war!"

It was past midnight.
"Not now," I said. "Sleep on it."

"The angels will watch over her," he said,
pointing to my daughter.

He left by himself, hitchhiking south.
The cops arrested him
somewhere on Route One.

Days later I heard
he was in the mental health ward.
When I walked in, he was in a straitjacket.
He said his name was Captain Bragg,
and he didn't know who I was,
but he thought maybe I was his sister,
sent all the way from Virginia to spy on him.

Years later, I'd get notes from him
addressed to "My Dear Sister,"
with news of his work in a coal mining town,
tutoring math to the miners' children,
sometimes a drawing on the envelope:
a stick figure with wings.

On Finding an Old Photograph
Long After We've Parted

for Jeff

There we are, bride and groom, in a redwood grove,
you, every inch Prince Valiant, tall, fierce-eyed,
me with a wide green sash,
my dress flowing to the soft duff—
but studying this old photograph,
I'm not so much struck by our youth
as by the lack of what surely should be happiness,
a quiet smile or a naked look of joy or even fear,
but we hold our bodies stiffly away from each other,
and on our faces I see only strain.

The trees we stand under have seen drought,
drenching rain, lightning, and the sun
of that long-ago July is bright, the sky
a perfect blue—but where,
I wonder, is the warmth of your two hands
to make our promises more than simply words?

Everything that came later
is there, in our glances that don't quite meet,
the way we lean away from each other,
even while we say we will be together
through sickness and health
forsaking all others till death.

Coast Highway at Night, After the Dickens Class

Driving past Devil's Slide,
darkness blotting out the unreliable cliffs
and the headlong drop to the sea,
I'd turn on the heat, the radio,
and call up the brave heroines like a charm to keep me safe:
Little Dorrit, Florence Dombey, Agnes Wickfield,
they would not be afraid, I was sure.

The creeks would flash by,
and the empty beaches to the right
—Pescadero, Pebble Beach, Scott Creek—
beaches where I'd played as a child,
riding slippery logs with my brother,
and collecting handfuls of shells and rocks
that would shine like treasures when they were wet.

By the time I reached Davenport,
I'd be thinking of home.
I pictured my daughter curled asleep
on her bed full of stuffed animals, and my husband
impatient for my return, pacing the living room,
a man I loved, not in the simple way
of my heroines, but in a difficult, modern way.

Pulling into the driveway,
I'd try to imagine this life belonging to Agnes.
I'd try to see it with her clear vision,
but then my dog would rush out,
ecstatic at my return,
and I'd bend down for his haphazard dog kisses,
his absolute fidelity.

Natural History Guides

Lassen Volcanic National Park

We studied the guidebooks
as if they could save our lives,
learning the names of the trees
by the scent of their bark,
pressing our noses into the rough trunks—
one smelled like pineapple,
one like a vanilla milkshake,
one simply like dust and sunshine.

We read how deer sleep away the afternoons
hidden in the shelter of trees,
how staghorn moss and lichen
live together on the same twig,
each giving sustenance to the other.

But the books had no words to explain
what was happening to us,
how we could have made such misery
in this place of perfect order,
the knowable world.

In an alpine meadow,
bending to hold a flower between my fingertips
—shooting star—
I looked for you,
to show you,
but you were already gone.

Salvage

Nothing left to save, is how it felt,
as I drove to the new house,
the backseat of my car
piled with the last belongings from the old place,
not even in boxes, just thrown in hastily—
a tea kettle, some shoes, books, t-shirts,
a stuffed elephant from my daughter's room.

How could a marriage die so quietly?
No struggle, just a flattening out of hope.

Halfway there, at the corner of Clares Street and Capitola Road,
where a shopping mall was being built
on the old bulb farm,
was a rose bush, leaning on a cyclone fence,
in full bloom. I pulled over to look—
the pink flowers: wide open,
a scent like pepper and honey
when I leaned into them,
and, behind, a bulldozer, looming, idle,
the blade resting on the ground.

So I picked as many of the flowers as I could—
the bush would be gone in a day or two,
making way for the parking lot.
The afternoon traffic rushed by
as I bent the stalks back
to break them off, trying to avoid the thorns.

Once home, I put them in water,
but the petals slipped off, one by one.
They couldn't hold themselves together.

The color was like the inside of a seashell,
I thought, and tried to be glad
I'd picked them, even if
they were falling apart.
Tried to think I'd saved them
from what was coming.

The Code

Looking at my age-stained hands,
I'm suddenly remembering
how we'd write on each other's hands,
in ink, a simple code, ILU for I love you,
or your initials intertwined with mine, and we'd smile
at how hard it would be to scrub away
those messages before we had to go out
into the world, hoping
the other would forget and leave those marks on
for all to see—
and I think again
of those hard years, when we tried to fit our selves
into the other, how what we built broke apart
again and again, until finally it was
beyond saving—but now, long after it could matter,
I see those words we wrote
were true, though long erased.

In the Sierras, Without You

being here in the mountains you loved
the planet having turned again
to the day of your death
no matter all the years
since we were together
or that we both found happiness
greater happiness with others
I remember our time here
how in the evenings
we'd jump in the car
race for the vista points
armed with blankets and Junior Mints
to watch the sunset

and lying on the granite slabs
still warm from the day's sun
ignorant of all that was ahead
we'd watch
the mountains take on the alpenglow
the clouds suffuse with pink
fading too quickly to gray

the chill once the sun was gone
taste of chocolate
still sweet in our mouths

Advice

Driving home from work—
my mind half caught
in the essays I'd been reading,
half lost in thoughts of a man
who seemed to have simply arrived,
though he'd been my friend for years,
only now he was saying
"Be with me," and I was afraid—
right there at Soquel Drive and Park Avenue
as the left arrow turned green,
I heard a voice in my head,
a male voice, one I'd never heard,
saying clearly, loudly,
Give him a chance.

I drove home, tried to shake it off—
after all, I didn't go around
hearing voices in my head!—
but the certainty didn't fade.
This was advice I couldn't ignore.

And I didn't.

Meteors

We were falling
Like meteors, dark through black cold
Toward each other . . . .
  —Kenneth Rexroth, "Inversely, as the Square
   of Their Distances Apart"

Reading Rexroth in the still-dark
of a Northwest winter morning,
my husband of nearly forty years upstairs, singing,
"Three silver rings, on slim hands waving," a song
about a lost love—going over the verse, again and again,
till he gets it right—

    and whether it's the poetry
or maybe those lines in the song, I can't say,
but there I am, back on that beach,
a long-ago summer—

    the chill of the night,
as we shivered in the sand dunes,
trying to shelter from the wind
and the ragged histories of our lives,
told in bursts, while the meteors
rushed out of Perseus,

    and no doubt
that we'd be sleeping in each other's arms
that night, as, staring up at the sky,
we lingered till we could no longer put off
the walk up the hill to my room,
the inevitability of our lying down together
bare skin to bare skin on that narrow bed
and what would follow—

those fires still opening, then dimming,
in the wide-open sky overhead.

Bottom of the Vineyard

for my husband, Fred Winterbottom

It made no sense then,
so long ago, and long before
we found each other, when a man I'd loved
wondered if we might have a future together
and asked a fortune-teller
what she saw. She said, "There's someone
in your way, standing
at the bottom of the vineyard."

It sounded like an old fairy tale,
or pure nonsense, something easily discounted.

But when I met you,
and you told me the origin of your last name—
from German, *the bottom of the vineyard*—
I remembered that woman's words,
and how she saw you waiting, faithfully,
all those years before,
at the end of a long row of dusty vines.

IV.

On Remembering

El Paso to San Francisco

After three days on the train
from Mexico City, then the bus
at the border in Texas, heading west,
it felt like I couldn't see anymore.

How strange not to care
what was outside the window—
the gas stations, diners, lonely front porches—
all passed in a blur of indifference.
And my fellow passengers, no fascination
with their untold stories, and that too was strange.

Even the girl just opposite me with the baby,
jostling her on her lap,
holding her up to see outside—
Look! Look!—but in her jeans
and shapeless sweater,
she looked too young to be a mother,
and I didn't want to wonder
what she was leaving or going towards.

Trying to appear worldly and jaded
instead of scared and tired
and barely eighteen,
I pulled an apple out of my pack
and bit into it—
not even registering
the mushy tastelessness of Red Delicious,
so different from the apples in our orchard at home,
still over a thousand miles away—
the sharp peel catching
in the back of my throat.

Bed and Breakfast

Bourton-on-the-Water, England

She wheeled a tea cart
to the sunporch, saying,
"Here, you must be tired from your travels.
I will leave you."

Did she pour the tea
before she left? That part
I don't remember—
just that her hair was piled
on top of her head.
She wore a hand-knit sweater—
blue, I think—with little knots in the pattern,
and a plaid wool skirt.

I never knew my grandmother,
but I wanted this woman to be mine,
felt maybe she *was* mine.

Afternoon sun on the field outside.
The strong hot tea, buttered scones,
raspberry jam. Rooks hopping in the stubble,
black and important, the plate
on my lap painted not with roses,
but with vegetables—
ears of corn, radishes,
carrots with their feathery tops.

Even then, all those years ago,
I knew:
hold on to this.
Keep it safe.

The Garden on Spring Street

Carrying the last armload of belongings out to my car,
I walk through the garden in twilight.
The tall purple stocks leaning into the path
brush my legs, releasing their sweet heavy scent,
and I think of all the time I spent
not just working in this garden,
but looking around, seeing how the colors
fit together, where I might add more blue or yellow—
and how my mistakes,
like planting tall plants in front of shorter ones
or putting in bulbs too late in the season,
were forgiven, and things always came out right.

I'll miss you, I say in my mind. *Goodbye!*
Then something, not quite the hand of a child
or the soft muzzle of a dog, comes back at me:

Goodbye!

And as I take one last look,
the plants have lost their distinctive colors and forms,
just shapes now in the falling dark.

For Mary in Yosemite

We perched on granite boulders,
the hot metal bowls warming our hands,
stretched out our tired legs,
and after the first bite, looked at each other, amazed.
"Can you *believe* how good this is?" you asked,
but it wasn't a question.
It was an exclamation.

This was after the four-mile hike
up the switchbacks from the Valley,
our full packs digging into our shoulders,
legs burning as we strained to keep up
with the others in our group, far ahead.

The air smelled like Jeffrey pines and warm dust,
and nearby, a mountain chickadee whistled
its descending three-note song:
fee-bee-bee! *fee*-bee-bee!

"We *have* to remember this!" you said,
pointing to the macaroni and cheese,
but now, forty some years later—
long after your sudden, too-early death
the following summer—
I'm remembering not that meal we shared,
but how, the next morning,
we got up before first light,
our jackets pulled tight against the mountain chill,
to see the hang gliders
leaping at sunrise from Glacier Point:

and now that you're gone,
I see how intently you watched them
run to the cliff's edge,
then jump off—no hesitation—as if
they were absolutely certain
those invisible currents of air
would hold them up, no question
those wings, made of nylon and metal,
could ever fail them.

My Friend's Brother

Only by chance I hear
of your death–since after all
it was your sister
who was my friend,
and she herself dead
so many—uncountable—
years ago.

I remember our greetings
in the halls, both of us
hurrying to classes,
your tall frame leaning forward
as you rounded a corner.
Your voice like hers
as you said hello.

Last time I saw you
you said you'd been having
long conversations with her
in your head ever since
she'd died— taken
so suddenly—no time
for goodbyes or to
set things right. There were
things you needed to ask,
you told me,
and things you needed
to say.

I picture you now
behind whatever curtain
the dead slip through
finally sitting down with her
and able to say
and to hear

what was needed
for so long—
the conversation deep,
full as a river
during snowmelt,
high in the mountains
you both loved.

Night Class, Santa Cruz

for my students who worked at the Wrigley's gum plant

Barely out of their plastic coveralls and headscarves,
these women would slip into the classroom
and sit together, near the back,
feeling, they told me, old and out of place
among the eighteen-year-olds.

No time for dinner before class,
but they didn't seem to mind, bending over their books
as if all the nourishment they might need
could be found in those pages.

They'd been taking care of others
for a long time—children, sick or absent husbands—
paying the rent, buying food, keeping things going,
and now they were trying for something more—
jobs where they wouldn't have to stand
eight hours over machines
mixing the Doublemint or Juicy Fruit,
where they wouldn't always feel the prickle
of sugar. "It seeps into your skin,
your hair," they said. "It gets inside you.
You can never scrub it off."

I don't remember their names now,
so many years later, but I remember
their careful handwriting,
out of practice since high school.
I remember hoping what I taught them
would get them closer to the lives they wanted,
feeling the weight of that,
as notebooks open, pens uncapped,
they looked to the front of the room
ready to take down every word.

On Devil's Gulch Road

Deer may have been *stamping in the glades*
in Rexroth's poem, but here, on this old fire road
leading to his cabin, all is quiet,
a stillness unbroken except by our footsteps
as we walk side by side
through steep meadows of dried oats, greasewood,
and purple-topped thistles.

Off to one side, the remains of an old orchard—
just one scraggy pear tree still standing,
its trunk pockmarked by woodpecker holes,
moss covering the unpruned branches.

We try to see it all through his eyes—
"he would have come this way," we tell each other,
wondering at that—only soon, our thoughts
turn more prosaically to lunch, back at the car.

The only other hiker, a man with a dog—
going fast as he walks in, the way we came—
gives us a brief nod in passing
before hurrying up the road.

We walk out slowly, still hoping for something
beyond the afternoon itself—
the dry smell of the grasses, a small wind
bringing up whirls of dust at our feet,
the blue California sky above, the generous years
of our long friendship. All this is enough,
of course, more than enough.

Constellations at 8,000 Feet

for Ellery, Caples Lake, California

A cold night in the mountains,
and our flashlights are dim,
flickering, as we make our way
to the shore and find a place to settle,
wrapping ourselves in wool blankets
pulled from the beds in our cabin.

"Look!" you say, as we lean back
to take in the sky
with its ten thousand, no, ten million stars
closer than I've ever seen them,
humming with their own existence.

I can't find any order
in all this blur of abundance, but for you,
these stars have been steadfast companions,
comforters in times of sadness,
and you hand me your binoculars
to show me the "W" of Cassiopeia,
the curve of Scorpio's tail—
and then I see my childhood friends,
the Big and Little Dipper.

Shivering, I'm soon ready to return
to the cabin and my book,
away from the urgent demands of the night.

The lake is dark, and small waves
rustle near our feet. Each breath
so deep, then as we exhale,
visible for a moment in the air before us.

April, Pinnacles Road

Pinnacles National Park, California

Seven cattleguards on the narrow road—
and clattering over each of them in turn,
it was impossible not to recall the fairytales
I'd spent my childhood reading, for yes,
one was clearly going deeper and deeper into a place
utterly separate from the artichoke fields
and the vineyards I'd passed on the highway—
and then, seeing, suddenly,
the jagged line of the Pinnacles,
rising up behind the farm off to the right
with its falling-down barn and faded house,
there could be no doubt. The steep rocks
sprung up from nowhere,
like a magic trick you gasp at every time.

I write this now, a thousand miles away,
looking out at a conifer-covered mountain,
and though it's spring here, the branches
of the big-leaf maples are still bare,
the new leaves not yet unfurled,
daffodils the only color besides green—
and this is as it should be,
but I'm remembering the rumble of the cattleguards
under my tires
as I'd drive in, hairpin turn by hairpin turn:
the sun-bleached grass,
and then the California poppies, sky lupines,
the tiny yellow flowers called goldfields
blazing on the hills.

Something Wild

for my daughter

What I remember is the hot desert air
on our faces as we leaned on the corral railing
watching the mustangs—bays, pintos, chestnuts—
mill around, restless, their eyes watchful,
not trusting, some with foals running at their sides
like shadows. They'd been brought in—
"gathered" was the word in the brochure—
for adoption. Twenty-five dollars
and a six-foot fence, and you could
take one home.

We took turns picking out
the one we'd most like
to gentle and make our own—
though of course we weren't going to do it—
couldn't, you with a baby, and me with a job
far from here.

Out in Antelope Valley, near your land,
there was a band of wild horses—
just a few, maybe four or five.
They'd appear in the distance sometimes,
on the far hills—easy to spot in that treeless landscape—
and, looking up from hanging laundry,
or loading the car for a run to town,
we'd watch till they were out of sight,
impossible to look away, our own fences
what held us in, forgotten for a moment.

Selling the Reno Land

Goodbye, Rubyhill, and all those pine seedlings
that couldn't survive the wind and heat,
roses eaten to the ground by jackrabbits,
daffodils that didn't ever come up,
house that was not built
on the rise facing the mountains. Goodbye
coyotes, locusts, artemisia.

What I owned was not you,
but the dream of a life I never entered:
wide open mornings, the sun—
before the brutality of the midday heat—
tinting the edges of the Dogskin Mountains
as I stepped outside to breathe in that cold desert air.

With or without me,
each year the desert peach
will spring forth from dry thorns
like some sort of Biblical miracle,
and the wheeling stars
will trace out a blessing
over that land—though I won't be there
to receive it, to look up, amazed
at the nearness of heaven
in such a place as that,
softening those hard edges
I have turned away from.

Collecting China

for my mother

it was after she died
that I found myself
going into second-hand stores
to look at the china

to lift it
turn it to the light
to want it
in an almost physical way

I'd never cared before
about this passion of my mother's
for dishes
but now I was lost to it

so that a teapot with a pattern of intertwined violets
a buttercup Spode plate
or a Haviland cup
almost too frail for a human hand

became things I needed to possess
always the promise of setting the table
for a meal she might attend
even though she couldn't

it wasn't something I could explain
I didn't understand it myself
I knew perfectly well
she wouldn't be lifting a cup of tea
to her lips or taking a cookie
from a flowered plate
or searching with me

in Goodwill or Salvation Army
for that amazing treasure
among all those chipped discards
from other people's lives

but I needed to bring
these finds home
give them each a place
of honor on my shelves
say to my mother
can you believe
what I found

A Kiss Before the World Ends

Corralitos, California, 1992

That was the summer we took comfort
in disaster movies—floods, earthquakes, ticking bombs—
don't ask me why.

We'd stretch out on the bed
in the cool downstairs room,
and while the floodwaters approached, say, London,
the seismograph began jerking spasmodically,
or the clock on the bomb moved ever closer to zero,
the main characters found time
for repartee and flirtation.

Young and good-looking in their crisp white lab coats,
they'd cast longing glances at each other,
as they sparred over the best approach
for saving the world.
The fact of possible annihilation
was mere backdrop for their own drama.

We'd be screaming, "No, no!
Save the world, you idiots!
You can flirt later! This is not the time!"

But, of course, we loved it,
being utterly safe, able to lose ourselves
for a couple of hours
in this pretend-disaster, pretend-fear.

Our world was so peaceful then, so settled.
Stretched out comfortably together,
we escaped into those near-death scenarios,
those distant others, right on the brink of losing it all,
and let the evening air
wash over us like a benediction.

Sometimes a deer might venture right up to the window
and look in, surprising us
with its wide-eyed wonder
at the strange human world.

Visitation

You cannot see anything until you are clear of it.
    —Henry David Thoreau, "Autumn: Journals"

Yes, take that time in Arizona,
sleeping on a pull-out couch
in the pitch-black living room of the casita,
my daughter asleep in the other room,
all quiet, all still—
then my parents, both long dead,
were in the room. They perched
on the armchair, draped with my clothes
from the day before. What were they
doing here, I wondered, as I struggled
to sit up. Would they
never leave me alone? When I asked,
they said they'd missed me.
They wanted to see me, was all.

I could tell that was so.
They didn't need anything from me
or expect anything back. Their love,
so complicated in life, was simple now.
They looked old and hopeful,
sitting together on that messy hotel chair,
and what I felt for them
was also simple. Just love.
How long were they there?
Impossible to say, and also not possible
to recall if words were spoken—but then
they were gone.

I slipped out through the sliding glass door
into the desert night. The air
was cool on my face, the stars
against the deep deep black, luminous.

There were no answers out there,
but the questions also
were gone. Only this vastness,
this sense of enough.

Insomnia, Again

I no longer put myself on that wide ledge at Pinnacles
when I can't sleep
but last night in my cabin
a thousand miles to the north
looking out the skylight at the welter of stars
so many so close-packed
they were indistinguishable
one from the other
my heart racing
though I couldn't work out why
I thought again of my old cure
picturing myself in that spot
where so often my friend and I
had stretched out comfortably against the rocks
pulled sandwiches from our daypacks
and talked about anything everything
the red cliffs of the Balconies rising up before us
and if we were lucky
the prairie falcon that nested in the cliffs
might swoop out right before our eyes
and always the turkey vultures
soared overhead in ever higher circles
till they were just black specks in the sky
before disappearing entirely
and again I felt myself stepping easily into air
not shrinking back from the edges
as I do in my waking life
but trustfully putting one foot out
then the other
and then falling
like a feather from a bird's wing
into sleep

On Remembering

I listened to you breathing
I wanted to remember the sound of your breath.
—W. S. Merwin, "The Sound of Forgetting"

Still dark out, I wake slowly.
Even the cat still sleeps,
a warm lump curled into my leg,
and, having slid into you in the night,
I relish the warmth,
the familiarity of your flesh against mine,
and know the sharp need to hold it in memory,
yes, to memorize it, as the poet I read last night
does the morning—so many
poems about morning
in this book written as he approaches ninety,
nearly blind,
hearing the rain against the broad leaves
of some Hawaiian tree
and remembering his childhood
in a much different place,
those rains, *those* trees, *those* mornings—
knowing even memory
won't hold them steady against time.

Swimming in September

Lake Whatcom, Washington

With summer at its end, no more
children's sand buckets or toy trucks
left behind on the beach from the day before,
we walk down to the water,
then step in, first cold, then almost warm,
a quick plunge, then swimming,
you saying, always, "It's not that cold—
downright tropical!"

The close-by mound of Reveille Island,
covered in fir trees right to the water,
and across the lake, the farther shore
draped in a low-hanging mist, sun
burning through the edges, lake water
soft against our bodies, your happy face
as you swim closer to shore—this
is what it's come to, then,
both of us nearly seventy-five,
and forty of those years together—
still, the wonder of it,
the day, new, barely begun,
as we rush out of the water for our towels,
tingling with aliveness.

Not Yet

not yet while the blackberries
are still just flowers and the pink bramble roses
hang off the corner of the garden fence
in a heavy tangle no
not yet as I sit in my friend's backyard
and the image of the black truck
on the wrong side of the road returns to me
speeding toward us
and unseen birds call back and forth
from treetops or the air
while off in the distance
a weed whacker starts up
and even that is a reason to stay
and the eucalyptus fill up the sky
the sun warm on my face
with another morning
not yet
the world outside beckoning
look at me here don't go

V.

From the 49th Parallel

I Contemplate Change While Reading *Bleak House*

I dip into this tale of displaced children,
orphaned, waiting on their fortunes,
this summer of my own displacement.
"The house has sold," my husband tells me,
his voice hollowed out by the phone.
"We have to be out in sixty days.
When are you coming home?"

I only make it through a few pages each night,
while darkness settles in outside the cabin,
and boats anchored in the bay pivot on their chains,
swinging with the tide and wind.

What do they have to say to me,
these children drifting through their lives
with little else but hope?

With the darkness, fear washes over me
as I think of my own life—
my friends, my garden, the students who kept me anchored
from one day to the next.
What will sustain me now?

I have no answers, so I turn back to *Bleak House*,
and though not everyone gets a happy ending,
Esther Summerson, who expects nothing for herself,
marries the man she loves,
and this, and the halyards
banging out a rhythm on the aluminum masts
of the tourists' boats in the bay,
lull me finally to sleep.

An Old Story

At fourteen, I had to sell my horse
and leave my home behind,
heading to the unknown—
another country, remote, far north—
with my brother, sister, my parents.

And though I returned later,
it went deep,
this leaving everything behind.

At sixty-nine, again,
I left my home
and traveled north, sun giving way
to fog and bursts of rain
before we got there.

I started a new garden
in a climate I didn't understand.
My tulip bulbs rotted
in the soil before spring.
The things I thought I knew
didn't apply.

I reached back for answers,
and found those pioneer women
I'd so admired as a child were there,
sitting on the rough planks of the wagons,
trying to take in the empty hills,
the vast openness
that so excited the men.

I imagined them listening
for something over the groan
of the wooden wheels on hard dirt—

it must have been the beginnings
of home, wondering
if there might be a stream
flowing beside the house,
not yet built, or if a shelf could be made
for the blue teapot
so it would always be there,
in plain view.

Last Time

Beforehand, I kept going over how it would feel
to know I wouldn't be coming back: I rehearsed
driving down the road—my road—
where so often I'd watched the sun
illuminating the moss on the live oak trunks from behind,
so they seemed to be glowing from within,
and then the cool of the deep redwood canyon,
leading to the apple orchards, town,
and finally, the highway.

But when the moment came, I felt nothing.
I drove out fast, the cat in her carrier
crying as we lurched over the speed bumps,
and the only thing I longed for was for this time
to be safely in the past. To be looking back
from somewhere else, years from now.

So much for last times.

Only now, I remember the last time
I said goodbye to my daughter's father,
not knowing he'd be gone when I got home,
and I wouldn't see him again, not for years,
and by then it wouldn't matter.
How easy to part with him that way,
just an ordinary kiss goodbye,
ignorant of what was ahead—no way
to know how his desertion
would suck me out inside till I felt doubled over
with hollowness, with shame.

Or saying goodbye to my father
who could no longer speak, but who clutched at my hand,
when I spoke words I could never say
when he was fully himself—and the next day
we heard he'd died in his sleep—*I love you.*

So remembering the crying cat, the hot car,
the unsaid goodbyes, I reach back now—
though the gesture is imperfect—
to embrace what's gone.

Unremarkable

I'd be lying if I said
I knew at the time, but now
it's clear—that moment
walking back to the house from the laundry room,
hot August sun on my back,
a full basket of clothes in my arms,
carefully stepping
from one rough paving stone to the next,
the overgrown garden on one side,
a tangle of sweet peas and blackberry vines,
a wild meadow on the other,
I knew—couldn't not know—
I'd be leaving,
no matter how much
I loved this place, how badly
I wanted to stay.

It was there, contained in that moment—
so unremarkable, so easy to forget—
one foot poised over the stone,
the basket heavy and awkward.
full of unimportant towels and t-shirts.

The Chinese trees of heaven
might have rustled, or the redwoods
at the base of the meadow
lifted their heavy boughs,
but that is lost. A Steller's jay,
flash of deepest blue,
might have shrilled a warning
but I didn't notice.

On Becoming Rootless

Even in winds that shake the house,
the western red cedar and Douglas fir
stand firm, only their upper trunks swaying
like the masts of ships in a strong swell,
and though the branches whip in the turbulent air,
the trees are solidly rooted, as I have to say,
I am *not*, each breeze tossing me aside
as if, like the dandelion seeds children blow on
to send their wishes into the world, I had become
insubstantial, nothing to anchor me to the earth.

Fault Lines

San Andreas, Loma Prieta, Cascadia Subduction Zone

we'd be shaken awake by our parents
when the house rumbled
and shivering
run outside till it was over
only moments but it felt
like it would never stop

I grew up like this
the earth alive underfoot
restless

later I moved with my husband
into a place
on top of the Loma Prieta fault

the landlord said it was safe
more than most

seismologists assured him
all the tension had been released
in the big earthquake
a year before
when the house had split apart
fallen off its foundation

but for now all was calm
and we lived there happily
for a long time

now here we live under the shadow
of an active volcano
and a fault line under the ocean
that experts warn
will cause a huge earthquake
in the next century or maybe the next week
no one can say

once the guppies were thrown to the floor
and lay there gasping

I'll never forget how
we scooped them up in the fish net
and dropped them back into the tank
where they floated on the surface
as if dead before darting away
alive again maybe more so
than before

Early Morning

sometimes the morning light
strikes the big maple
just outside the window
from behind
so the moss on the trunk
seems to glow

I count those mornings lucky

and remember something
from Dorothy Wordsworth's journal
about how the sheep
in the distance
when the sun was just right
would have a rim of gold
outlining their bodies

I imagine her stopped
just watching for as long as she could

sitting in bed looking out
I'm glad for that astonishment
hers and mine
and that what we see
every day
could make us stop
look again

could make us ask
what was that

At the Barn View Community Garden

We must cultivate our garden.
        —Voltaire, Candide

I cannot tend my garden
without trampling on something
so I walk gingerly here, trying not to hurt anything—
yes, I admit my garden lacks order or method:
nasturtiums surfing over the broad leaves of the pumpkins,
clarkia and bachelor buttons happily choking
the tomato plants, eager rhubarb
shading the strawberries, who themselves
have run rampant past my allotted boundaries.

"Some plots look untended," we've been cautioned.
"Please take care of your gardens!"

When I look around,
I see that my fellow gardeners have trained their beans
to grow up poles, or have kept the dinosaur kale
in perfect rows, and I realize I must
do something, make a stab at tidying up.

But for now, I pick a few cherry tomatoes
and some dahlias to put in a vase at home—
huge blossoms, deep purple and shaggy orange!—
spray water over the mass of leaves,
and, with the August sun on my back,
feel happy in this small wilderness
of my creation.

The Birds at Lake Louise

It was loneliness that brought me to the birds—
those daily walks around the lake
puzzling over the waterbirds, the mallards, of course,
old friends, but then beginning to know others, the
    goldeneyes,
buffleheads, the thrill of an occasional wood duck with its
    elegant markings,
and out on the log in the middle, always, one or two
    cormorants,
those ancient birds, descended straight from dinosaur times,
often holding out their wings to the sun to dry.

And as spring approached, tentative, as if feeling
as uncertain of its welcome here as I did myself, suddenly
the bushes along the lake were noisy with songbirds,
and I began learning their names—song sparrow, spotted
    towhee,
dark-eyed junco, and the red-winged blackbirds with their
    watery song
weaving between the other notes, holding them together.

What I saw was a whole world, all these lives,
so occupied with their own concerns—territory, nesting,
    mating—
but nonetheless allowing me a glimpse inside, and it was like
those parallel lines left in the wake of the swimming ducks,
how they'd linger for just a moment on the surface
before disappearing into the body of the lake,
and I watched this from the shore,
mesmerized, forgetting I was alone.

Missing Orion

I never really learned the stars
as I should have
only a few of the easy ones
the Big Dipper   the North Star   Orion
but they became companions
and now living in a deep conifer forest
I miss the open sky
of my old house
and especially I miss
Orion who seemed to always
meet me as I stepped outside
in the middle of the night
to breathe out whatever bad dream
had awakened me
breathe in
the good cold night air
listen to the reassuring shuffle
of deer in the meadow
and look up
for my friend
splayed bigger than life
across the night sky
mighty hunter
with his shining belt of stars

Rain in Fall, Remembering Santa Cruz

The cedar boughs drip with rain,
and though it's just September,
the maples are already turning.
With a sharpness that startles me,
I remember the smell of eucalyptus
in the town where I used to live.

After a storm, the pavement
would be littered with their seed pods
and their crescent moon-shaped leaves.
I'd go down to the beach
to walk the familiar path, feel the freshness of the wet air,
take in the smells of the beached bull-whip kelp,
the dank ocean, sometimes dead seabirds washed ashore.

I can see how the Chinese poets, so often writing in exile,
knew this ache for what's far away,
even as they wrote from a garden with blossoming plum trees
or a mountaintop overlooking a prosperous valley
where all was in order, all was good,
seeing only that it was not the other place,
the one memory would not let go.

From the 49th Parallel

Bellingham, Washington

So far north here, sometimes
it feels like we're teetering
on the very edge of the Earth
and into the region the ancient maps
called Terra Incognita.

Hard to get a solid footing.

Chill wind through the giant trees
that have seen it all. The branches
of the western red cedar
with its delicate tracery of needles
lift and fall
like a ragged breath.

On the Way to Town

Driving down Lake Louise Road, through the conifer forest,
sword ferns lining the banks, suddenly, up a rise,
there's the farm, green field, chickens wandering free,
the red barn, like a barn in a child's farm set,
yellow house set back on a knoll, apple trees in front—
all so perfect I wonder if it's quite real, and if,
in some future time, I'll remember this particular
turn of the road and be filled with longing for it,
even as now, driving past, I'm thinking of another road,
missing the way it curved through oaks and redwoods,
how it opened to a clearing, the same way
this one does, like saying *all will be well,*
no, *all **is** well if only you'd look, here it is*—
heat blasting through the air vents—and now
the barn, the field, in my rear-view mirror
disappearing behind me.

Studying Italian with Fred

There's nothing Mediterranean about these Northwest winters—
snow piled up a foot deep on the back deck,
the birdbath iced over—
but we open our textbook, with the jaunty title *Ciao!*,
you in a heavy sweater, me with a blanket over my legs,
the furnace on, and the fireplace giving out its flicker of cheer,
and take on the day's lesson,
a dialogue about a couple ordering food.

The photo shows them seated outdoors,
dressed lightly, a sleeveless dress, a t-shirt,
sun full on their smiling faces,
as they place their orders for *spaghetti al pomodoro*
and *bistecca con insalata verde*, and ask for *un mezzo litro
di vino rosso*. I can't help noticing
how young they look, and carefree,
as they wait for their food, laughing over a joke
that isn't included in our *dialogo*.

You take the part of Gianni, and I am Lucia,
and soon we're there in the *ristorante*—
never mind that we're both in our seventies,
and it's the middle of winter,
never mind that the only sun of the day
has just glimmered through the tree branches
a half hour before dark—we've escaped
into the intricacies of this language,
where Gianni can say to Lucia,
ho una fame da lupo, I'm as hungry as a wolf,
and she knows exactly what he means,
no translation needed.

Tai Chi at the Sudden Valley Y

"Wave hands like clouds," we're told,
 and dutifully, we hope gracefully,
 we wave our hands—one hand the cloud
 moving over the other, the earth.

Anyone walking into this drafty room
 might say we're a motley group—
 and so we are, all over sixty, in our stocking feet,
 some wearing parkas and gloves
 to ward off the chill—wavering
 on the one-legged poses,
 some kicking higher than others,
 not always in step.

But when we stand quietly
 before the close, holding still,
 feeling the stillness,
 having parted the mustang's mane,
 strummed the lute,
 and driven the monkey back,
 something has happened.
 Our faces shine with it.

As we step outside, real clouds are scuttling
 over the evergreens,
 and the hills are dusted with snow.

At Lake Louise in October

I could fancy that a thread of vital light became visible.
      —Virginia Woolf, "The Death of the Moth"

Watching the last of the spring birds
flying into the willow thickets beside the lake—
and the mallards who will winter here
swimming in pairs across its surface,
I feel the threads of connection
from their lives to mine,
and thinking of those I've loved
and those I still love,
I feel the tug of that thread
invisible as a spider's traveling line in shadow—
seemingly fragile, but tough—
shimmering as the sun breaks through.

Wild Swans on the La Conner Road

Unwearied still, lover by lover
　　—William Butler Yeats, "The Wild Swans at Coole"

You might say there's nothing other-worldly,
nothing symbolic here
in this flooded field by the road—
not quite Yeats' wild swans
to be carefully counted off in pairs—
but just hundreds of white birds
grazing like a flock of domestic geese,
long necks bent to the green winter grass
as we drive past
on our way to celebrate your birthday,
and nowhere safe to stop for a better look.

Only a rush of beauty in passing,
gone before it could really be seen.
But enough to say, "Did you see that?"
And then, "Can you believe
all these years together?"

How the time flashed by.

BARBARA BLOOM is the author of two previous collections: *On the Water Meridian* (2007), a finalist for the Northern California Book Award; and *Pulling Down the Heavens* (2017), both from Hummingbird Press. Bloom is a four-time winner of the Sue C. Boynton Poetry Contest in Bellingham, and her poems have been featured on the radio on *The Writer's Almanac*. Her work has appeared most recently in *Catamaran*, *Adventures Northwest*, and *Western Washington Poets Network Anthology*.

photo: Kelly Carbert

Bloom grew up in California, but when she was a teenager, she and her family moved to a remote coastal homestead in British Columbia, where their survival depended on learning to operate a boat, fish, hunt, and grow their own food. Though she returned to California to finish her education, this experience of living so close to nature was profound and continues to inspire both her work and her life.

Bloom earned an M.A. in English and creative writing from San Francisco State University and taught composition and creative writing at Cabrillo College in Santa Cruz, California, for over thirty years. She has a grown daughter and two grandsons and lives with her husband in Bellingham, Washington, where she teaches writing workshops through Whatcom Community and Continuing Education.

SHANTI ARTS

NATURE · ART · SPIRIT

Please visit us online
to browse our entire book catalog,
including poetry collections and fiction,
books on travel, nature, healing, art,
photography, and more.

Also take a look at our highly regarded art
and literary journal, *Still Point Arts Quarterly*,
which may be downloaded for free.

www.shantiarts.com

www.ingramcontent.com/pod-product-compliance
Lightning Source LLC
Chambersburg PA
CBHW070332090426
42733CB00012B/2456